USING SOCIAL SCIENCE KNOWLEDGE

IN BUSINESS AND INDUSTRY

Published for

THE FOUNDATION FOR RESEARCH ON HUMAN
BEHAVIOR, Ann Arbor, Michigan

USING SOCIAL SCIENCE KNOWLEDGE IN BUSINESS AND INDUSTRY

Report of a Seminar

Edited by

RUTH LEEDS

Instructor in Sociology
Reed College

and

THOMASINA SMITH

Human Factors Specialist
System Development Corporation

1963

RICHARD D. IRWIN, INC.

HOMEWOOD, ILLINOIS

First Printing, June, 1963

Library of Congress Catalog Card No. 63–16887

PRINTED IN THE UNITED STATES OF AMERICA

Preface

THE MATERIALS in this book originally were presented and discussed at a seminar held by the Foundation for Research on Human Behavior at Gould House, Ardsley-on-Hudson, in April, 1962. Previous Foundation seminars reporting and discussing new research on organizational behavior, leadership, and management had indicated clearly that many problems in using social science knowledge in business and industry bear no relation to substantive research findings. It therefore seemed logical that a discussion of research and theory about the *use* of social science knowledge in business and industry would strengthen the bridge between producers and the prospective users of social science research.

The focal point of the seminar was the presentation of materials by:

John Paul Jones, General Manager, Organization Development, Union Carbide Corporation;

Paul Lazarsfeld, Professor of Sociology, Columbia University;

Floyd Mann, Professor of Psychology and Program Director, Survey Research Center, University of Michigan;

Herbert A. Shepard, Professor of Behavioral Science, Case Institute of Technology; and

Goodwin Watson, Professor of Psychology, Columbia University.

However, in preparing this book, the editors felt that a summation and a reorganization of the research and discussion into topical chapters would be more useful to the

v

reader than a series of sections reporting each leader's presentation and the discussion by other participants. In doing so, the identity of individual contributions has been lost, although the colloquial style and figures of speech which reflect the actual discussion at the seminar have been retained. To the discussion leaders who have allowed their thoughts and research to be reorganized in this way, the editors express their thanks.

In addition to the five discussion leaders, an active group of business participants took part in the seminar and contributed appreciably to the ideas reported in this book. Seminar participants are listed at the end of this volume.

The editors especially would like to thank Professor Paul Lazarsfeld of Columbia University who read an early version of this book and made helpful comments. They also want to thank the Foundation staff, including Dr. Hollis Peter, chairman of the meeting; Dr. Sven Lundstedt, who organized the seminar with him; and Miss Margaret Bush, who gave assistance in preparing the book. Finally, the editors are indebted to the seminar participants who loaned their notes, answered questions, and provided valuable ideas in informal discussions.

RUTH LEEDS
THOMASINA SMITH

Table of Contents

I. Introduction

BUSINESS FIRMS have traditionally operated with reference to a mechanistic model, concentrating on the improvement of machinery, the development of more efficient production methods, and the manufacture of better products, to attain their goals. The input to which business and industry paid the least attention was the human factor; employees were quite literally viewed as "hands." Shortly after the turn of the century Frederick W. Taylor began to think about more effective ways to employ human beings; he treated man as a physiological system, and concentrated on the problem of how his physical energy could be used most effectively. Taylorism or scientific management did make a great contribution to more effective utilization of the human factor, but it had its limitations; it did not prove to be the hoped-for panacea of business.

During the early thirties the wage laborer began to be seen as something more than a machine which happened to be alive. The turning point came with Elton Mayo's attack on the traditional view that a worker responded to management on a completely individualistic basis, and the view that money was the only incentive that could motivate him to produce. The experiments conducted by Mayo and his associates in the Western Electric Company marked the genesis of the concern with the worker's social environment and his social well-being. Thus if business and industry were to attain their goals more effectively, they would have to concentrate on the development of their human resources, not as machines or atomized individuals, but as social beings.

Although business and industry had flirted with the social sciences prior to World War II, following the war's end, the courtship began in earnest. For business and industry needed answers which the social scientists could provide, and the social scientists, for their part, needed research sites in which useful findings could be developed. During the seventeen years that the businessman and the social scientist have worked together many problems have emerged, for the application of social science to industry proved to be more complex than was thought initially. Today the businessman wants to know precisely what social science can offer him, and how its contributions can best be applied. Moreover, he wants to know with a fair amount of precision what differences the application of social science knowledge will make in the operation of his company. And the social scientist for his part wants the opportunity to conduct his research properly, so that he can develop a body of scientific knowledge and can offer the businessman findings which have undergone adequate testing.

Mutual Needs of Social Science and Business

In order for social science application to effect significant changes in the business world, the social scientist and the businessman must establish a viable relationship with each other. The social scientist must have a clear understanding of the businessman's problems, and the businessman must have an understanding of what the application of social science entails. Social science is not a commodity that can be purchased at the local appliance store and then installed like a television set or a refrigerator. Second, since the social sciences cover almost the entire gamut of human behavior, the social scientist must specify to the businessman which aspects of his discipline are useful to the latter. The social scientist has to indicate in what circumstances social science might have something to offer, and also, the limitations of social science knowledge. Finally, if the application of social science is to yield concrete results for the businessman, it must be translated into specific courses of action which he can follow.

This report focuses on the general question of what the social sciences can contribute to business. It is divided into three sections, covering the social scientist–businessman relationship, the uses of social science in business, and the implementation of social science knowledge in the business context. This report, then, is not substantive in the sense that it considers specific problems of business and industry which the social sciences might solve. For example, the reader will not find a description of how the application of social science knowledge mitigated the adverse social effects of the installation of automated equipment in a company. What the reader will find is a consideration of factors underlying the actual use of the social sciences, factors which must be accounted for jointly by the businessman and the social scientist, in order to permit effective application of social science to business and industry.

The several social science disciplines—psychology, sociology, and anthropology—are treated together under the phrase "social science." Although these disciplines differ in their methodology and in the primary questions they seek to answer, their actual use by the businessman entails similar problems. A viable relationship must be established between the businessman and the social scientist, whether he is a psychologist, sociologist, or anthropologist. The findings of all three disciplines must lend themselves to translation into specific courses of action. Thus, regardless of substantive differences, the three disciplines must come to grips with similar problems if they are to make significant contributions to business and industry.

II. The Social Scientist-Businessman Relationship

THE ISSUE of applying social science knowledge in industry extends beyond questions of what are appropriate methods, what is the status of social science, and what kinds of contributions social science can make. The relationship between the client or user and the consultant or social scientist partially determines the success of attempts to apply social science knowledge to industry, and must be considered along with more technical matters of methods and techniques. The businessman and the social scientist represent two occupational groups with divergent values and goals, who must work out effective means of interaction and coordination in order to apply social science knowledge successfully to the problems of business organizations.

In the first part of this section the factors which contribute to or militate against effective working relationships between the businessman and the social scientist will be discussed. Differences between the occupations *per se* and the perceptions of one occupational group toward members of the other which effect the nature of their working relationship will be considered.

The second part of this section will deal with some role relationships that have been established between social scientists and businessmen. Several examples of successful and unsuccessful working relationships between the two occupational groups will be described.

PROBLEMS ARISING FROM THE DIFFERENT OCCUPATIONAL REQUIREMENTS OF BUSINESSMEN AND SOCIAL SCIENTISTS

Many problems arising from the social scientist–businessman relationship can be traced to differences in values, goals, and perceptions of the two occupations. Each occupation represents a different world, the world of industry versus the world of academia, and the forms of communication and ways of thinking in these worlds do not necessarily coincide. Some persons maintain that the differences between these occupations are irreducible, and unless this is assumed and taken into account, problems will inevitably arise.

What are the characteristics of each occupation that account for problems in the social scientist–businessman relationship? What are the expectations and perceptions of each vis à vis the other? First, the characteristics, perceptions and problems of the social scientist vis à vis the businessman will be discussed. Second, we turn to the problems of the businessman in relation to the social scientist from the businessman's perspective.

Social Scientist—a Marginal Man in Business?

The social science consultant or researcher to industry frequently feels like a marginal man with his simultaneous relationship within two worlds. Within the value system of the academic world he has chosen the less respectable alternative of applied rather than pure research. Because of this the academic community often looks at him with suspicion. Frequently the consultant or researcher is in conflict between loyalty to his profession and the demands it makes on him (such as publishing in scholarly journals), and his desire to participate in the business world by consulting, leading seminars, and doing research.

This conflict is intensified by the problem of overselling versus underselling social science. Social scientists feel that their disciplines can contribute to industry, but they are not always sure that what they give or the way in which they give help will be useful to industry. They do not want to offer something they are not prepared to deliver or to make promises when they are uncertain about the usefulness of their knowledge.

For the social scientist located in a research bureau connected to a university there is additional strain. University professors think that consultants are "selling" themselves and even impart this attitude to their students. In addition, the status of the consultant in the research bureau is somewhat precarious. He does not have the security of professional tenure or a guaranteed salary, necessarily. Many of his research projects are dependent on outside sponsors for financial support.

The social scientist who is employed as an inside practitioner in industry is also somewhat marginal. Personnel departments in business are already suspect as staff groups with little influence, and social scientists associated with them are frequently considered softheaded by businessmen. The insider's loyalty to his employer and to the organization can come into conflict with his loyalty to his discipline and profession. For example, one inside practitioner was told that he was not hired to do research or run a lab but just to provide psychological services. The questions he was asked frequently required long-range studies in order to answer them, but he was not allowed the time or resources to do the research. His professional standards could not be satisfied because of the constraints imposed by his employer.

The social scientist who is committed to the value system of his academic discipline comes into conflict with the opposing value system of the organization where he works. He can become frustrated because the value systems are not the same, so he may try to change the value system of the organization. He fails to realize that it is not necessary to have identical value systems in order to work out an effective working relationship with his employer, and that satisfactory relations can be established by sharing values which are mutual, respecting differences and mutually educating and enriching the other to his point of view.

The social science practitioner within a company may also be cut off from his discipline and from sufficiently frequent contact with his professional colleagues. Both communication with his discipline, and the contributions he can make to his profession, are hampered.

One aspect of this problem is discussed in an article on the emergence of "crypto" social science in industry.[1] Crypto is used in the sense of true but unrecognized material and refers to the large quantity of organization staff studies that are never incorporated into the body of social science literature but remain in the files. Much systematic research of high caliber done by inside social scientists remains unrecognized and lost to the discipline and hampers the relationship of the scientist with his profession.

Differences in Value Systems

Other sources of strain for the social scientist consultant arise from his values and goals. An example of this is the polarized political orientation of the two occupa-

---

[1] Robert Carlson, "On the Prevalence of Crypto-Social Science Research in Industry," paper read at the Association for the Study of Social Problems, August, 1961.

tions. Politically, social scientists tend to be somewhat less conservative, whereas businessmen tend to be more conservative. Moreover, the more eminent social scientists tend to be even less conservative than their lesser known colleagues. These eminent social scientists are also the ones most likely to consult for business since business is interested in employing the top leaders of a discipline. This polarization of political orientation can lead to value conflicts between the two occupational groups.

An example of conflict between the values of the social scientist and the business world is the case of a psychologist who did a research study on managers of a public utility. He found that these managers were working long hours and lived for their work. As a psychologist and a human being, he was concerned about the kind of life they were leading. However, the president of the company did not want him to raise this issue because he thought it in the best interests of the company to have exceptionally hardworking managers.

Inadequate Training in Application

Few social scientists have been trained to apply their knowledge in a field situation. Physicians, in contrast, spend a great deal of time applying their book knowledge to concrete situations by treating patients through an internship program. The only equivalent program for the social scientist to give him an opportunity to apprentice in the field is the program in behavioral science at the Case Institute of Technology. That program is very new, however. In general, social scientists do not know how to do social engineering in order to work effectively in industry and make contributions to it. Many social scientists do not have their knowledge internalized so that they can use it in action situations. In effect, some are unable to practice what they preach.

Not only do social scientists lack training in social

engineering and in applying their knowledge in a field situation, but many of them think that social science data alone are sufficient to convince managers to introduce organizational changes. The social scientists assume that social science facts and findings, when presented to the businessman to justify the introduction of an innovation into the organization, will automatically suffice for the businessman to decide in favor of the social invention.

They do not take into account what they should already know as social scientists—that the businessman has his own philosophy and theory of human behavior which many differ from the more formal theory of the social scientist. The businessman's assumptions about the way people behave are the bases on which he evaluates programs, makes decisions, and relates to his employees. When the suggestions of the social scientist conflict with the manager's theory, data contrary to his theory may not be enough to convince him. He may feel on the basis of his experience that the data of the social scientist are wrong in some way. For example, a manager may have the theory that he must have either adequate policing and regimentation in a unit or chaos. This theory may make him unwilling to experiment with less traditional means of control. The social scientist then has to provide an experiment in a context where the system is not policed and there is no chaos. But experimental data alone may not change the manager. In such a case, it is necessary to modify the manager's theory of human behavior in order to convince him.

Social Scientist's Ambivalences toward Businessmen

The perception of businessmen by social scientists should be considered in attempting to understand the problems that members of the two occupational groups have in their interaction. What are some of the general attitudes of the social scientist toward the businessman with whom he works?

Social scientists sometimes resent business leaders on prestige grounds. Trustee boards seldom contain professors among their membership though they always include businessmen. The businessman when asked why professors are excluded will say that many deans and presidents of colleges and universities are on various boards. However, professors do not view college deans and presidents as professors but instead as the managers of the university who run its business similar to the manager in the industrial firm. Professors feel they have no power positions in the community. They feel that the community will leave the education of the children to them but will not assign them positions of power in the community.

In many cases the social scientist is ambivalent toward the businessman. On the one hand the businessman makes more money than the social scientist so he may be seen as materialistic and greedy. On the other hand, the businessman does make it possible to lead a more comfortable and pleasant life. In addition, the social scientist in his saner moments admits that many businessmen are concerned with more than profit and loss statements. Social scientists who have worked with businessmen often express surprise and pleasure at their intelligence and breadth of interests.

Different Goals and Time Perspective

The businessman is oriented toward coping with situations which call for decision making and action on a daily basis. The manager's model is the income statement and his primary criterion of success is the profit and loss statement. The social scientist in comparison focuses on research and the answering of questions, and in some cases is unconcerned about practical applications or policy actions. To the businessman, the goals of the social scientist do not always appear to be furthering the ends of business.

Another problem in the businessman–social scientist relationship arises from their divergent time orientations.

The businessman, though he may realize the need for long-range studies to answer some of his questions, usually works under the time pressure of coping with situations on a short-term basis. He cannot wait years for data since he is making decisions daily. The social scientist, on the other hand, is not oriented toward working under the same short-term time pressure. He usually needs a long time to formulate and test hypotheses and to collect and analyze data—his research methods themselves are predicated upon a lengthy time span. Furthermore, the social scientist is usually less concerned with the utilization of his research findings than with developing an understanding of human behavior and theories to account for it. This differential time orientation of the businessman and the social scientist is often a source of conflict.

Related to the time orientations of the two groups is the problem arising from the time lag between the installation of a social invention or innovation and the point at which it is reflected on the profit and loss statement. When a social invention or experiment is introduced into an organization, the social scientist consultant is neither able to guarantee what the results will be nor the length of time it will take for the results to become visible. He knows that these two factors are largely beyond his control and depend on people in the organization.

This poses a problem for the businessman since he is responsible for ensuring that organizational innovations will ultimately be reflected favorably in the profit and loss statement. In many cases, he is unwilling to take the risk of experimenting with social inventions when the time lag is unknown. The businessman is likely to be more willing to take a calculated risk in the development of new products in physical research than in social research with which he feels less familiar. But he may be missing an opportunity to introduce important social innovations that would be advantageous in the long run to the company and would produce significant changes.

Social Science Seen as Inconsistent

In many cases, the businessman has difficulty understanding the contributions made by the various disciplines of social science. Psychologists, sociologists, and anthropologists all seem to be writing about the same things, but saying quite different things. Even within the same social science discipline, much of the material to which he is exposed seems to contain inconsistencies or contradictions. The businessman can point, for example, to widely different sets of management principles advanced by psychologists as representing social science knowledge in this area. How can he be expected to believe that any of these findings are scientific when there is apparently so much disagreement among social scientists?

Communication Difficulties

Communication problems can arise from the specialized technical language used by the social scientist. The manager finds it hard to understand the technical vocabulary, and is reluctant to delve into anything that seems so academic. Unlike physicists, chemists, and engineers, the social scientist has few counterparts in industry. The physicist who publishes a highly technical paper for his professional colleagues finds that many people in industry can understand and use his material. The social scientist, however, finds that his technical articles are read and understood by relatively few businessmen. Only when academic material has been translated into his parlance and popularized in business journals will the businessman read and consider using the information.

For this communication difficulty the social scientist is only partly to blame. Some researchers are guilty of long-winded, fuzzy writing filled with jargon. More commonly, however, social scientists are simply attempting to describe new phenomena, to make necessary distinctions between related concepts which are lumped together in popular language, and to communicate precisely with other social scientists.

Related to the manager's reluctance to read academic material is the attitude of the businessman toward the expertise of the social scientist. Some businessmen are intimidated by what they regard as "expertise." At the same time, many managers, unconsciously and intuitively, use good social science principles and show considerable ingenuity in solving applied problems in the social field. But they may often think that the social scientists will regard this as trivial and unimportant because formal terminology and rules were not used; consequently they may react defensively in their relationships with social scientists. Another frequent business attitude is suspicion toward those social scientists who seem to have knowledge but do not practice what they teach.

Professional Standards and Ethics

Social science has few legal mechanisms for licensing or providing other means by which outsiders can identify legitimate practitioners. There are no easy ways by which businessmen can distinguish the honest and competent social science practitioners from the charlatans. Even in the years since World War II the proportion of incompetents and fakes offering services to industry in the name of social science has been great. The businessman often cannot distinguish his friends from his enemies. Many managers who in good faith employed charlatans were badly burned by them, and are understandably reluctant to expose themselves again.

Some young social scientists who have recently completed their Ph.D.'s appear to enter industry waving their degrees like witch doctors brandishing their magic wands, lacking humility, and thereby alienating many business-men. In view of their inexperience the problem of integrity with regard to the privileged information the social scien-tist gathers from employee interviews may arise here. Un-less the social scientists protect the anonymity of respond-ents, they could be viewed as part of the control apparatus of the company and feared by employees as a research arm of the boss. The ethics of using interview material or other social science data to affect the careers, or in other ways to harm interviewees, should be of as much concern to the businessman as it is to the mature social scientist.

Another problem of integrity arises when the inside social scientist or the outside consultant feels that he must give management the "popular" answers, the answers that he knows management wants to hear, rather than giving the "right" answers based on his best professional judg-ment. When the social scientist gives popular answers which later experience shows to be inadequate, the social scientists' knowledge and skills, and perhaps his integrity, become suspect. In the long run then, the social scientist can destroy the very role and field that he is trying to build up for himself within the organization.

Need for Careful Use of Data

Another problem occurs from the use of data collected by the social scientist in the organization. The social scien-tist with his need to test theories (particularly in the measurement area) enters the organization, makes surveys or experiments, and collects his raw data. In those unfor-tunate cases where the social science–business relationship ends at this point and where the researcher leaves the un-analyzed data with management, management may still try to use these data as a basis for making action decisions.

Frequently, these unanalyzed data are misused by the manager. This misuse of data is the fault of both the social scientist and the businessman. The social scientist has failed to tell management the state of the data or the conditions under which they should be used as a basis for decision making. Management on the other hand has made its own interpretation of the data without knowing their potential usefulness or the situations in which they could appropriately be applied.

An example will illustrate this point. A survey of employees made by a researcher showed considerable dissatisfaction with the communications from top management. Without analyzing what the real needs were, the company redoubled its communication output to employees via its company magazine and then blamed the original research when a later survey showed no decrease in employee dissatisfaction with communications.

ROLE RELATIONSHIPS BETWEEN BUSINESSMEN AND SOCIAL SCIENTISTS

In order to understand the problems involved in applying social science knowledge to industry and to illustrate the ways in which social science has been successfully implemented in an organizational setting, the relationships between the producer and the user of social science knowledge must be examined. The social scientist, as a researcher or as a consultant, provides the knowledge, while the businessman or practitioner is the prospective user. In the following pages several examples of working relationships between social scientists and businessmen will be described. Instances of both successful and unsuccessful relationships will be given to show that the kind of relationship that is established affects the extent to which social science skills and knowledge have been applied to the problems of business organizations.

The Disappearing Social Scientist

One kind of relationship between social scientists and businessmen which has been found to be unsuccessful is that in which the social science consultant is trained to "become part of the furniture" in an organization. In some early studies in industry, social scientists were trained to enter an organization to make their objective study of organizational behavior without being conspicuous or interacting to any extent with members of the organization. In their attempts to study organizational behavior objectively, they also learned the skills of becoming ineffectual and unnoticed. Many of them succeeded so well that they had no impact on the organization.

Studies would be made by the social scientist, but there were few attempts to implement the findings in the organizational setting. In addition, there was infrequent interaction between the social scientist and the businessman which hindered the development of a coordinated working relationship between them. Lacking a good working relationship, the manager had little opportunity to learn from the social scientist or to increase his understanding of the potential contributions of the social scientist.

How Much Dependency?

To what extent should the businessman be dependent on the skills and knowledge of the social scientist consultant? In those relationships in which the businessman becomes dependent upon the social scientist and his skills, and fails to incorporate social science knowledge into his everyday operations within the organization, the businessman is not being helped very much by the social science mode of thinking. On the other hand, the businessman is expected to have some degree of initial dependency on the

social scientist who possesses certain knowledge and professional skills which are needed to help the businessman
solve certain organizational problems. If the businessman
were not somewhat dependent upon the social scientist,
there would be no work for the social scientist in industry.
On the other hand, if the businessman remains overly dependent on the expertise of the social scientist, he is failing
to incorporate the new ideas and ways of thinking from
social science into his own philosophy of management
which underlies his day-to-day actions as a manager seek-
ing to improve his organization.

From the social scientists viewpoint, an overly dependent relationship is one in which the social scientist
helps an organization by contributing specific research
studies and advice, but where no attempt is made to teach
the manager social science skills and knowledge so that
he can use them himself. This kind of relationship is unsuccessful in the long run and leads to a relatively ineffective use of social science. For example, when the consultant
leaves the organization there is the problem of fade-out.
In such cases, the effects of the researcher or consultant
on the operations of the organization tend to wash out over
time since better ways of applying social science skills and
knowledge were not learned by the manager or others in
the organization. The existing philosophy of management
has not been altered and everyone operates as he did before
the consultant entered the organization. This is not to
suggest that the businessman must learn all the special skills
and expertise of the social scientist in order to avoid per-
petuating a dependent relationship with him. It means only
that unless the manager or others in the organization adopt
the social science way of thinking to some degree and/or
improve their behavioral skills, there can be little lasting
gain to the businessman or to his organization from ex-
posure to social science.

The Detroit Edison–Survey Research Center Program

One example of a successful working relationship between businessmen and social scientists is that of Detroit Edison and the Survey Research Center of the University of Michigan. The relationship between Detroit Edison and the Survey Research Center has existed continuously for fifteen years and can be described as a symbiotic relationship in which both organizations have profited from their mutual association.

Detroit Edison is interested in supporting social science research and in using social science data to change and improve its organization. The Survey Research Center views Detroit Edison as a field site for conducting a series of studies on organizational behavior. Both organizations have similar interests in studying organizational change and there is common agreement on the use of the scientific method.

There are differences in values and goals between the Detroit Edison managers and the University of Michigan social scientists. The social scientists are more interested in pure research, precise measurement, and rigorous scientific methods than are the managers. The managers are more concerned with improved production, a more effectively functioning organization, and a brighter profit and loss statement than are the social scientists. In the beginning of the relationship, extensive time was spent to reach an understanding of the values and goals of each group. There was a process of mutual exchange and clarification of the expectations, aspirations, and values of each. Though the goals were different, it was recognized that respect for the goals of the other was necessary in order to work together.

The social scientists explained their methods, research goals, and research problems. In turn, the managers gave the social scientists insight into the organization, described its power structure, and discussed their experiences in the organization.

The social scientists felt responsible for their actions since the relationship was to be an ongoing one. They were not going to do one study and leave. Therefore, they did not conduct experiments or use methods that would disrupt the organizational machinery.

The social scientists learned that mutual participation in research activities improved the quality of the relationship. They made an effort to see that management, line people, and the union participated in research projects. They asked employees who were involved in a study for their suggestions and ideas. Data were fed back to the participants at the completion of research projects. For example, before beginning a study of several different plants, the researchers tried to obtain contingent acceptance for the proposed study. They made a postcard survey to determine attitudes toward the study. In addition, they talked to employees on all shifts and asked them for their ideas. Finally, they reviewed the proposed project with the union and with a research committee made up of plant managers and supervisors.

The relationship was continually worked on by both the businessmen and the social scientists. Both groups knew it was important to develop mutual trust. Both groups considered the relationship as a learning process and there were no expectations that the social scientists had magical formulas or panaceas.

Both assumed that facts alone were not enough to bring about change within the organization. The social scientists did not limit their activities to making studies and then giving the data to the managers. They used the process of feedback, in which research data were brought back to work groups and even to individual employees, as a means of utilizing the social science knowledge to effect organizational change. The process of feedback as it was developed and used at Detroit Edison is described in Chapter IV of this report.

Significant changes in the organization have resulted from the attempts to apply social science knowledge in a practical situation. Detroit Edison has been pleased with the changes in its organization which resulted in part from this continual relationship with the Survey Research Center.

In addition, the managers in working with the social scientists learned from them the social science way of thinking. The managers modified their philosophies over time and learned to utilize social science knowledge on a daily basis. At this point several generations of managers in some parts of the company have been exposed to the social science way of thinking; this is reflected in the quality of their relationships with employees and their behavior in the organization. Thus, not only have organizational changes been implemented through the activities of the social scientists, but the knowledge and skills of the social scientist have to some extent been acquired by the individual manager and employees. This has made it possible for the individual manager to become his own social scientist and to utilize social science in handling his organizational problems. Over a period of time, this has resulted in less dependence on the social scientist to make other studies and to contribute to new areas where his skills had not been utilized.

The social scientists have also greatly benefited from their relationship with Detroit Edison. They have had a permanent field site for fifteen years where they could continually study organizational problems of professional interest. The rare continuity of the relationship allowed them to make studies of long-term organizational change and collect a fund of data over time which is in some respects unique. They were able to do challenging research and publish technical material in professional journals. They not only accomplished basic research, but learned how to do social engineering, and how to help apply social science knowledge in an organization. The field site also provided an opportunity to train new researchers in survey methods, in applied research, and in applying social science knowledge to industry.

III. The Uses of Social Science for Business

SOCIAL SCIENCE can be roughly described as composed of two types of knowledge: (1) partially verified theories, concepts, and modes of thought to account for human behavior and provide a way of thinking about human behavior, and (2) a body of substantive findings which describe the behavior that has ensued under specified conditions and techniques for studying human behavior. Both aspects of social science are intimately related, each contributing to the development of the other; both, if *properly used*, can be of value to business and industry. Social science theory and concepts provide the businessman with a systematic frame of reference for thinking about his human resources. Many substantive findings of social science having analogues in business and industry can suggest to the businessman what the locus of a particular problem is. Techniques for studying human behavior can provide the businessman with specific data describing behavior in his company. We shall discuss these aspects separately, beginning with social science as a mode of thinking, but it must be stressed that if the businessman is to benefit from social science, he cannot make use of only one aspect. To be able to perceive the analogues between social science findings and business processes one must adopt what has come to be known as the social science mode of thinking, that is, to develop a sensitivity to the implications of conditions and processes which are often taken for granted. To assess if the application of social science knowledge to business has created a change for the better, its effects on human action must be measured.

A. SOCIAL SCIENCE AS A MODE OF THINKING

Social science as theory and as a mode of thinking can force the businessman to examine his own theories on which he premises day-to-day decisions. What are the assumptions on which decisions and actions are based, and what are the implications of these assumptions for future decisions and actions? Will the businessman's body of assumptions permit him to recognize problems which might be solvable, or will they only permit him to rationalize the status quo? In essence, adoption of a social science mode of thinking compels the businessman constantly to examine his theories, to readjust them, and to expand them as he gains more insight and experience.

Promotability of Informal Teachers

Let us proceed further by way of example. An unpublished study by the late Samuel Stouffer showed that many persons who occupied relatively high positions in industry and business owed their success to the teaching and training given to them by others in their firms. These "informal teachers," however, never attained positions equally as high in the hierarchy as their pupils. A facile explanation for this phenomenon might be that a person who is capable of developing the talents of others does not necessarily possess the requisite attributes which lead to promotion. Some businessmen might in fact entertain such a theory, but it is based on an incorrect assumption; namely, that all persons who are "promotable" are in fact promoted. But this is hardly the case. Sometimes persons are "promoted" to innocuous positions where they are "out of the way." Sometimes the proper person cannot be found for a given job so that a "nonpromotable" person is given it, and so forth.

The explanation that "informal teachers" lack attributes which lead to promotion does not hold on closer examination. This mode of explanation which depends on factors supposedly inherent in the person social science tries to avoid by asking instead: What factors inhere in the particular situation, in this case the training situation, which lead to higher promotion for the protege than for his teacher?[1]

One possible social science explanation for this phenomenon pivots around the concept of *degree of visibility*. "Informal teachers" are not promoted to high positions because they engage in activities which tend to be *intangible* and *invisible* to persons who make promotion decisions. Training an up-and-coming subordinate is not as easily perceived or measured as recruiting new customers to the firm, for example, so the former activity is less likely to be rewarded unless special mechanisms are developed to counteract the lack of visibility. In short, if management wishes to rely on on-the-job training to develop its human resources, it must institute mechanisms that allow training activities to be rewarded. Otherwise, the unanticipated consequence might occur that employees will ignore a

---

[1] Sociology and psychology are considered together under "social science" in this report. However, only sociology poses the question, "what factors inhere in a given situation which lead to certain actions?"

managerial dictum to train and develop talent since such activity is not visible, and so likely to go unrewarded.

The concept of visibility can be used as a cue in thinking about many problems which might arise in industry. Another example is provided by a problem which an English aircraft company faced during World War II. It continually found itself overproducing motors and underproducing frames. The difficulty was traced to the fact that motors in excess quantity could be stored underground while frames always had to be stored outside, thus making the number of frames produced highly visible to the public, in particular to any passing member of Parliament. If the latter perceived that frames were being overproduced, chances were that parliamentary funds to the company would be reduced. Therefore, the company's "safest" course of action was to produce less frames.

Managerial strategies can be built around visibility or a lack thereof. In the interests of management certain phenomena might best be left invisible while others should be made visible. The businessman who is able to judge when visibility is the optimum and when not, wittingly or unwittingly, is engaging in the social science mode of thinking.

Since this way of thinking existed long before the social sciences emerged, today's social scientists have no monopoly on it, although they constantly aim to refine it. Within business and industry, great managers are their own social scientists, and good ones at that. There are other managers who only think they are their own social scientists, but the theories on which they premise their decisions might be too narrow or contain erroneous assumptions. These managers, in particular, can be helped through training in the social science way of thinking. And the great managers might benefit through reassurance from social science that their way of thinking and their theories conform to what the social scientists have learned through their own work.

A Manager as His Own Social Scientist

The latter case is exemplified by a manager (to be referred to as Brown) who used social science knowledge intuitively, without recognizing the underlying logic, in dealing with a particular problem. At the time he became head of a particular division in his company, the research and development laboratory, the factory, and the engineering unit were physically separated, with no face-to-face communication between the heads of each. Also at this time there was concern about product quality. Brown felt that the entire division was responsible for product quality, not just a particular subunit, and that the undertaking of joint responsibility required face-to-face communication. Hence, he organized his division and, moreover, invited the union president to participate in the solution of the product quality problem. Through establishment of face-to-face communication among unit heads, Brown had virtually eliminated interunit fights over responsibility for the quality of the product; and by enlisting the help of the union president, grievances vanished from that production area for the next year. Brown perceived himself as a "system bucker," but, in fact, he had intuitively made use of several social science hypotheses in his reorganization. Once he was made aware that he had engaged in a respectable application of social science he felt reassured and less anxious about his "system bucking."

Brown exemplifies the manager who has internalized an intuitive knowledge of social science and its mode of thinking. Such internalization is the goal that managers and social scientists both must strive for if social science is to be of maximum use to business and industry.

Unanticipated Consequences

As yet, there are no hard and fast rules for engaging in what we call here the social science mode of thought. Therefore, we shall present a few more examples of it. Earlier, we used the phrase "unanticipated consequences"; like visibility, this is a cue phrase, which forces one to consider in greater detail the ramifications of an ongoing system.

An organization can be thought of as a system oriented toward the attainment of goals, for example, the maintenance of profit at a certain level. The organization itself is composed of subsystems, each with its own specific goals, the attainment of which is intended to further the general organization goals. In practice, however, it frequently happens that the members of a particular subsystem become overwhelmingly concerned with their own goals, to the detriment of the general goals. This represents an unanticipated consequence for the organization.

The Tennessee Valley Authority's program was watered down to a conservative level as a result of just such an unanticipated consequence. The TVA adopted the strategy of working through existing local agencies, such as the land grant colleges and the land agencies, to implement its program. In many instances, however, the TVA program conflicted with the goals of the local agencies. For example, the extension services of the land grant colleges were given, generally, to the white, more well-to-do farmers, not through a conscious policy of discrimination, but because these farmers were more likely to cooperate with the college agents. To the extent that the TVA had wedded itself to the extension service, it proved to help only the "upper class" farmers rather than the Negro or tenant farmers. Thus the TVA found itself modifying its program in a conservative direction which accorded with the programs of the local agencies, thereby defeating the original intention of Congress when it authorized the TVA.[2]

Another example of how a subunit can subvert the goals of the total system occurred in the cereal industry. Since cereal is, generally speaking, a child's food, its consumption decreases with age. If cereal consumption could be extended for one more year in a person's life cycle, greater profits would accrue to the industry. This has been pointed out many times by the central institution of the cereal industry; for competitive reasons, however, individual cereal companies persist in slanting their advertisement to children rather than to adolescents and adults, thereby diminishing the chances for extending cereal consumption for several more years in a person's life cycle.

Not all unanticipated consequences are detrimental to the system in which they occur. A positive unanticipated consequence of the automobile age was the elimination, for the most part, of typhoid fever. With fewer horses in the country, there were fewer flies to act as carriers of the disease. Our main concern here, however, is with unanticipated consequences that are detrimental. In business and industry, unanticipated, undesirable consequences cannot always be avoided, for they stem from decisions which an executive had to make. It becomes his task then to correct for those unavoidable, but undesirable consequences. (The TVA selected its strategy of working through existing local agencies in the hope of gaining "grass roots" support for its program, for it believed in democratic planning to avoid disruption of local folkways, and not in spoon-feeding the population. Also, the agency wanted to sidestep the red tape of a central government bureaucracy. Given its orientation, the TVA had to make use of existing agencies, but if it had been able to recognize potential unanticipated consequences, it might have been able to develop mecha-

---

[2] Philip Selznick, *TVA and the Grass Roots* (Berkeley: University of California Press, 1949).

nisms to correct for them.) To the extent that the manager is able to utilize the social science way of thinking, he might be able to mitigate the effects of undesirable, but unavoidable consequences.

An insightful manager who thinks as a social scientist might be able to locate the source of a problem, but he is unable to go further because he does not know enough about the factors in the situation which have generated the problem initially. Thus, he might sense that union-management conflicts stem from the nature of the actual relationship between the two parties, but beyond this he does not know what to look for. In this instance substantive social science findings can prove useful. But of special importance is the fact that unanticipated consequences can often wreck efforts to introduce and apply social science knowledge in organizations.

B. AN EXAMPLE OF THE APPLICATION OF SOCIAL SCIENCE FINDINGS TO INDUSTRY: THE CASE OF INTERGROUP CONFLICT

Oftentimes a new subunit is established within an organization to solve a particular problem. In many such instances management finds that although it might have solved one problem by creating a new unit, it has also generated new problems through its own creation. A classic example is the staff unit which is supposed to advise the line on better means of implementation, but instead, comes in conflict with the line organization.[3] Here, social science can help through its analysis of factors that lead to intergroup conflict.

---

[3] See Melville Dalton, "Conflict between Staff and Line Managerial Officers," reprinted in Amitai Etzioni, *Complex Organizations* (New York: Holt, Rinehart & Winston, Inc., 1961), pp. 212-20.

Sherif's Experiment

A by now classic experiment on intergroup conflict was conducted by Muzafer Sherif in 1949, at a boys' camp. Sherif was interested in testing several hypotheses concerning the nature of groups, one of which was as follows:

... if two in-groups are brought into functional relationship, positive or negative out-group attitudes and appropriate friendly or hostile actions in relation to the out-group and its members will arise, depending upon the harmony or friction between the goals of the two groups. The testing of this hypothesis also involves in prototype form the process of the rise of group stereotypes.[4]

At the outset of the experiment, the campers were allowed to form their own friendship groups; then these groups were pitted against each other in various competitions, which yielded data on intergroup relations in conflict. During the final phase of the experiment, Sherif attempted to bring the two groups into harmony, but found it almost impossible to destroy the conflict boundaries which he had created.

Experimental Conflict among Managers

As an outgrowth of Sherif's work, a similar experiment was conducted among management training groups at Esso.[5] "T" (training) groups were formed, whose members were permitted to develop feelings of cohesiveness. Along with cohesiveness, feelings of anxiety were gener-

---

[4] Muzafer Sherif, "Experimental Study of Intergroup Relations," in John H. Rohrer and Muzafer Sherif, *Social Psychology at the Crossroads* (New York: Harper & Bros., 1951), p. 398.

[5] *An Action Research Program for Organization Improvement (in Esso Standard Oil Company)*, published by The Foundation for Research on Human Behavior, Ann Arbor, Mich., 1960. See also Herbert A. Shepard, "An Action Research Approach to Organization Development," *Management Record*, June 1960, and R. R. Blake and J. S. Mouton, "Reactions to Intergroup Competition under Win-Lose Conditions," *Management Science*, Vol. 7, 1961.

ated as each group wondered how well it was performing, for in the initial phase the groups were floundering, and the members felt themselves to be inadequate for the task at hand. These various emotions and feelings combined gave rise to a negative competitive attitude, manifested by such statements as "Your group is worse than mine." During the second phase, the "T" groups were given an opportunity to act as problem-solving teams, each one being assigned to the same problem. Once solutions had been formulated, a spokesman for each group presented his team's solution in a court session where it was judged. The prospect of the court session evoked the effect of intergroup conflict. Each group's cohesion and morale increased; a high degree of task orientation prevailed; mechanical procedures were used to solve the problem under the guidance of dominant persons in each group.

Further effects were noted during the presentation of solutions in the court session. Objectively, the solutions were almost identical, and of equally poor quality. Each group, however, perceived its own solution as being radically different from, and vastly better than, that of the opponents. Each was systematically blind to any similarities and greatly magnified minor differences.

The spokesman himself experienced pressure to be a hero, to win a favorable judgment for his group by presenting the best solution. If he was committed to the solution and believed it to be the best, this pressure was less problematic. If he was not committed to the solution, however, the spokesman strongly experienced the group's pressure, for he could not become a traitor; at worst he was expected to be awarded a draw if he was unable to do the best, that is, to win for his group. Throughout the experiment itself, no spokesman betrayed his group by capitulating and saying that the opposing group's solution was better.

During the court session, each group perceived the spokesman for the opposing group to be malicious and muddleheaded; this perception extended to the opposition as a whole. Moreover, as the court session progressed, each group perceived its own spokesman with less and less respect, for it believed that he was presenting the solution inadequately.

Once the judges awarded a decision there were clear signs of victory and defeat. The victorious group, becoming complacent and cohesive, had difficulties returning to work. Its members perceived themselves as having no problems and talked of going home. The defeated group generated rationalizations to show that it really had not been defeated, and talked of ways to win the next time. Furthermore, the defeated group fractionated internally, with hitherto submissive members turning on the leader and blaming him for the loss. The judges were viewed as stupid, by the defeated team, and as having made the only possible decision, by the victorious group.

Consequences of the Experiment: Interunit Relations

The managers of various plants who underwent this experiment in intergroup conflict were able to see that the experimental situations corresponded in detail to phenomena occurring in their organizations. Problems stemming from bargaining committees and departmental loyalties, for example, took on added meaning and significance for these men which transcended the purely cognitive level.

Although the persons who undergo such training experiences are quick to grasp their implications for behavior in the plant, the actual gains from such sessions are small unless the organization to which a manager belongs is able to offer support once he returns. If the manager returns to a nonsupportive organization, what he has learned is unlikely to lead to any changes, and fades away in time.

Where the organization offers some support, however, a change can be effected as a result of such training experience. The experience of one participant in such a training experiment will illustrate the point.

The plant from which the participant came had an inefficient performance record with regard to the maintenance of automated equipment. A committee was formed to study the problem but was unable to reach a consensus on how it might be solved. One suggestion was to form a new division, but an existing division balked at the prospect of losing members to a new unit. Hence a compromise evolved which led to the establishment of a new section in the maintenance division which would service automated equipment and a new department in the engineering division which would develop and install new automated equipment. The liaison between the new units proved to be inadequate. In addition, the fact that a department has higher status than a section contributed to the poor relations between the two units. These factors set the scene for potential intergroup conflict, particularly since one division head hoped to undermine the compromise.

The training participant, who belonged to the maintenance section, upon his return from the experimental experience, discussed the problem with the engineering department head. The two of them invented some procedures for reducing the conflict potential. Consequently, each unit met to formulate its objectives in the presence of the other unit. Rules were promulgated concerning the joint meetings of the two units. Members of the section were paired with their opposites in the division, thereby establishing links across unit boundaries. These innovations helped to ease the strained relations between the department and the section by mitigating the potential for conflict.

Union-Management Relations

A more dramatic application of training in intergroup relations, although, generally speaking, applications of social science knowledge do not yield drama, was made in regard to union-management relations.[6] For ten years there had been bitter conflict between the two parties. During most of the time no union contract existed. Through a training program on intergroup behavior, management realized that its relationship with the union followed the classic conflict model, so it began to modify its behavior toward the union. The first step was to ask the union when it would like to meet rather than simply announcing that management would meet with union officials on a certain date. Second, management suggested that the two groups work together in framing their demands rather than separately as heretofore.

During the first nine months of the "joint" era there were many setbacks, compounded by the fact that management initially perceived the union president as being loudmouthed, while the union officials had little respect for management. Hence, management had great difficulty in restraining itself from reverting to former patterns of behavior. Through working together for almost a year, however, management gained respect for the union president and vice versa. By the year's end the two parties had arrived at a mutually agreeable contract.

In short, by consciously and systematically changing its behavior, management, in effect, led the union to make a reciprocal change, thereby changing the norms under which the relationship functioned. Of particular interest in this instance of applying social science findings to industry is that management's attitudes toward the union

---

[6] R. R. Blake and J. S. Mouton, "Union-Management Relations," in Conflict to Collaboration, *Personnel*, Vol. 38, 1961.

changed *after* it modified its behavior, and the union officials began to do likewise. This suggests that intergroup relations training and application of social science knowledge to a situation pays off, at least in most instances, only if the actual behavior is affected, not just the attitudes of the parties concerned. To state the matter another way, to broaden management's theories of action, and to sharpen its perceptions by alerting it to the social science mode of thinking is inadequate if this does not lead to changes in its behavior.

The Chronically Defeated Group

Another outgrowth of experiments with intergroup relations is understanding the problem of a chronically defeated group. The staff is frequently the chronically defeated group vis-à-vis line organizations. Because of its weaker position, the staff is more vulnerable to defeat and comes to expect it, which leads to a vicious circle of defeats. This is illustrated by a particular staff group that had as its head a man who was enthusiastic, authoritarian, and hard driving. He "called the shots" at all times, behaving the same way to people above him as he did toward people below him in the hierarchy. This behavior was acceptable as long as the demand for staff services was high. Once a few errors were made, however, and once there was less need for staff work, his tactics were no longer acceptable, and he left the company. His replacement was ineffective in that he did not maintain contacts with his superiors, and was not responsive to his subordinate's ideas. Consequently, the staff unit produced less and less. When a second replacement assumed the staff chief position he confronted a demoralized and downgraded group, having the syndrome of a chronically defeated group: (1) the best people leave the group; (2) other members would like to leave but are restrained by external factors; (3)

the group is no longer cohesive, having fragmented into individual isolates and small cliques; (4) the group itself is isolated from the rest of the organization in that its members keep to themselves; for example, they no longer have lunch with personnel from other units; (5) a paranoid atmosphere prevails in the group, with many rumors flying; communication between individuals is ineffective; interpretations of the same events tend to vary widely and to be distorted; (6) the group develops a "servant" image of itself, waiting for directives from above, and not assuming any initiative; (7) other units of the organization are perceived as competitors; (8) the group spends its time refining its internal bureaucratic machinery, thereby reducing informal contacts with the rest of the organization and increasing its isolation; (9) members of the group distrust each other, and lose respect for and confidence in each other's abilities.

The third staff chief was then faced with the problem of restoring the group to a level of confidence and security where it could once more be an effective unit of the organization. To this end he adopted the following procedures. First, staff members were interviewed by an outside social scientist to obtain the above report of the group's state. The report was distributed to each member with the request that he communicate his reactions to it. Many members of the group wrote long letters to the social scientist, in some cases agreeing with his report, in others, disagreeing. Significantly, many members had shown their letters to one another and had discussed the issues at length. This led to increased communication among the personnel on subjects which previously had been tabooed. Second, the social scientist wrote another report, recommending that action be taken in three areas of general concern: group objectives, group organization, and professional development. The staff chief then divided the group into teams of

persons who did not normally work together, and requested that they make suggestions for reorganization of
the group's structure and procedures. The changes suggested by the teams were then incorporated into the reorganization, without causing anyone to feel that his rights
or status had been violated, and so leading to a general
sense of relief.

A year later the group itself had not changed dra-
matically, with one exception—the suspicious atmosphere
had disappeared and members were no longer afraid of
each other. Moreover, events were no longer distorted.
The social reorganization of the unit was followed by
physical relocation, an event which is often threatening
and potentially explosive. But in this case, physical relocation was accepted without disturbance. No one felt that
his status was threatened through the change; no one attempted to impute meanings to it which were not there.
Had the physical relocation occurred before the advent of
social reorganization, it would have led to much distorted
discussion, hurt feelings and intensified paranoia. The
interviewing, the feedback of the report, the suggestion
teams, the social reorganization, and the physical relocation had all been designed to eliminate the syndrome of
chronic defeat. The fact that the physical relocation did
not create any disturbance indicated that the syndrome
had been successfully abolished.

Lack of Communication between Units

Lack of communication links between units of an organization is another typical source of intergroup conflict
which can be remedied through application of social science knowledge in this area. The links between organizational units serve to mitigate potential conflict, and where
such links are missing, conflict, competition, and chronically defeated groups emerge. This is illustrated by a par-

ticular organization which had no linking pin between its headquarters unit (HQ) and its several field units. It lacked persons who had dual memberships, either in two fields, or in one field and HQ. Given this organizational structure, if a field unit's performance is considered inadequate, HQ is likely to respond by replacing the field unit's manager. A second consequence is that the various field units are placed in competition with each other. For example, HQ at one point was contemplating a new investment in one field unit. It requested each of four units, all of which were in need of new investment, to make an economic study to determine whether or not it should be the locus of the new investment. Each returned a glowing report to HQ explaining why it was the most appropriate unit for added investment. HQ thereupon requested that the units restudy their needs and turn in additional reports, which proved to be even more glowing and tailored to the desire for investment than the previous ones. Moreover, each unit thought that it was certain to receive the investment. Since so many vested interests had emerged in regard to the outcome of HQ's decision, HQ selected a fifth unit, which had never made a report, for its investment site. The four units reporting originally had been left deprived; their one consolation, if one can call it that, was that members had developed a high degree of commitment to their respective units as a result of competing for the investment.

Intergroup conflict is particularly detrimental to a decentralized organization. Ideally, each unit manager should give priority to the corporate interests, and not to the interests of his own particular unit. In reality, however, managers tend to give priority to the welfare of their own units. For example, they do not relinquish jobs to other units which might be able to perform them better. Figure 1 illustrates a common headquarters-field situation.

FIGURE 1.

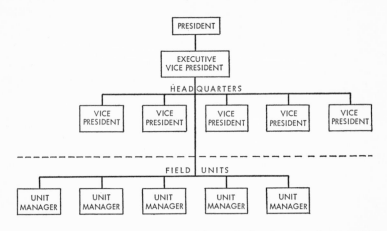

The executive vice president feels that he has a HQ team, but does not perceive that this might include the field managers even though the charted relationship suggests that field managers are part of the team. Each field manager sees himself as king of his particular realm, rather than as having one position in an organizational hierarchy. Kings engage in similar activities, and so do field managers; but just as kings do not share secrets of state with their opposites in other lands, so the field managers do not communicate with each other. HQ perceives itself as the source of policy while the field units mobilize the energy for implementation, and there is a one-way street from policy to implementation. Furthermore, HQ operates on a divide and conquer theory, not perceiving the field units as a totality. Consequently, the field units do not exchange ideas with each other on how HQ policy could best be implemented, and rarely communicate with HQ about the ideas they are implementing. In many instances, these ideas, innovative in nature, backfire because of unanticipated consequences, and at such times in particular, field managers hesitate to report to HQ that all is not well in their realms. HQ uses a "decentralized" theory of organization thought to be quite adequate for its purposes but which in reality may prevent adequate action for the attainment of organizational goals.

There have been a number of experiments on improving HQ-field relationships.[7] The following is an example of work done by the behavioral sciences group at the Case Institute of Technology: HQ and field personnel were brought together for a week of laboratory training sessions. The laboratory design called for the establishment of a HQ team and a field team. The organization's president and executive vice president each had a turn at being the leader of each team. To resolve HQ-field misunderstandings and conflicts, the social scientists present instigated cycles, whereby the two teams would come together at regular intervals for joint discussion of key issues. As a result of coming together, pluralistic ignorance was reduced among the field managers; they found that they shared similar attitudes toward HQ, and that they had similar problems. This also helped to mitigate competition between the field units. Each group spent some hours developing its image of the other group, and information on these images were exchanged.

Although HQ felt that the week's training programing represented time well spent and the field personnel was enthusiastic about the experience, the results still left something to be desired. First, through working together the field managers had developed some bonds with the president and executive vice president. A follow-up program is necessary, however, if these bonds are to be maintained over any length of time. Second, the vertical line between HQ and its field units did become a reality, but

---

the concepts and organizational theory which HQ employed were relatively unaffected by the week's experience.

The term *decentralization* is misleading for it implies a dearth of collaboration, yet it is precisely close collaboration which is needed if the organization is to function more effectively, if field managers are to have more success with their revised implementations. Collaboration can only be effected if HQ changes its concepts and theories, but, as stated, such a change did not occur.

This concludes our examples of how the findings from studies of intergroup conflicts can be applied to business and industry. Our examples of applications have run the gamut from being highly successful (the section department example, the union-management example) to moderately successful (the chronically defeated group), to barely successful (the HQ-field example). Much of the success of the union-management case is attributable to management's efforts to restrain itself from reverting to former behavior patterns. This suggests that if social science findings are to be of maximum use to business and industry, management cannot relax once it has completed its training course but must continually strive to put into practice what it has learned.

C. SOCIAL INVENTIONS

To apply social science findings to a problem requires in some instances the development of a "social invention."[8] One social invention is the paired relationships formed to minimize conflict between the section of the maintenance division and the department in the engineering division in our first example of the application of intergroup conflict

---

8 Herbert A. Shepard and Robert R. Blake, "Changing Behavior through Cognitive Change," *Human Organization,* Summer, 1962.

findings. Another social invention is the reorganization in the chronically defeated staff group. In short, "social invention" is a convenient phrase to designate new ways of organizing persons around a given task. Many organizations today suffer from the fact that their structures are not well suited to the tasks they are trying to perform, as was the case with the organization having a HQ field relationship problem; hence the need for social inventions.

Historically, social inventions have "evolved"; that is, they have not been introduced consciously with the intention that they will meet certain requirements of the organization. The structure of a television show production exemplifies such a social invention. Within the television world (and other forms of show business for that matter), continuous coordination and cooperation are required among personnel if the job is to be completed. The staff performs its jobs in a state of high tension. Sometimes the tension is aggravated by a star who acts like a prima donna. During work breaks and after the completion of a production the staff relaxes completely, often lying down. Such complete relaxation permits release of accumulated tensions, thereby mitigating the possibility of open conflict during the work phrase, which would be completely detrimental to the job at hand, disrupting needed near perfect coordination and timing.

Similar if not greater precision of coordination and timing is required at Cape Canaveral. Quite possibly the Canaveral technicians also relax completely during work breaks to release pent-up tensions. Observations such as these could lead to the general statement that work break facilities and activities should be devised to compensate for human problems, like a high degree of tension, which are an outgrowth of the work situation. The emergence of such tensions represent unavoidable but undesirable consequences for which compensation can be made through the invention of appropriate work breaks.[9]

Another area which illustrates the need for conscious social inventions is that of education. Although, in general, important discoveries in science are made by younger rather than older persons, during the last sixty years relatively fewer discoveries have been made by younger scientists. This has been rationalized frequently with reference to the increasing complexity of science and the increasing amount of knowledge which students have to assimilate, thus leaving them little time to make discoveries. Such rationalization, however, blinds one to the possibility that the present-day bureaucratic structure of educational institutes blocks rather than creates opportunities for youthful discoveries, and that there is a need for social inventions here. A teacher of high school biology who took students with him during his summer's research discovered that they were capable of making original contributions.[10] A further set of experiments has recently been conducted at Case Institute of Technology with entering freshmen working as research teams in a complex field of modern science, demonstrating another set of conditions and opportunity structures under which young people can make scientific discoveries and contributions. The problem of appropriate opportunity structures is a generic one, and the question which the social scientist must ask is what structures and what settings are most appropriate for the effective accomplishment of specified tasks.

---

[9] Such phase movements of groups, from work to work break, have been studied by R. F. Bales, "The Equilibrium Problem in Small Groups" in Talcott Parsons, *et al.*, Working Papers in the Theory of Action (Glencoe, Ill.: The Free Press, 1953). Pages 111-61. See also R. F. Bales, "How People Interact in Conference," *Scientific American*, March, 1955.

[10] Frederick R. Avis, *A Documentation of Twelve Years Experience on Science Summer Programs, 1949-60.* Worcester Foundation for Experimental Biology.

To be able to discover appropriate social inventions, the social scientist must continually view the structure with which he is concerned as a system, where what happens in one unit implies consequences for what happens in another unit. And even if the businessman himself is not in the business of social inventions, he too must think systematically if he is to make a decision which implies the fewest unavoidable but undesirable consequences for his organization as a whole.

We have now come full circle. The first use discussed to which a businessman might put social science was a mode of thinking to guide his day-to-day behavior to broaden the theories on which he premised decisions, to make him aware of the consequences of necessary actions, and ways to correct for them. But a mode of thinking can only bring the businessman so far; eventually there comes a time when he realizes that he lacks information which his mode of thinking requires if he is to make the proper decision. At this point social science findings become relevant. The realization that there might be another side to the coin of union-management relations, for example, does not suffice to effect changes in one's behavior. One needs to know what aspects of behavior have to be changed and in what way. But changing his behavior can oftentimes bring the businessman only a little closer to the solution of a particular problem. The problem might have its genesis in an inappropriate social structure. At this point there is need for social inventions, the clues for which are inherent in social science theory and findings.

Although we have presented what might be considered the three major uses of social science for the businessman as a progression from mode of thought to social invention, the three are in many instances intimately related. The HQ-field units problem is illustrative. HQ held an inadequate theory of organization behavior, which led to a minimization of cooperation and collaboration between itself and the field; on the behavior level this was abetted by an inappropriate structure—the lack of linking pins between the field realms and HQ. All three factors—mode of thinking, behavior, and structure—need to be changed in order to eliminate intergroup conflict and competition. This much is evident. The precise strategy for effecting change, however, is not so evident given the present state of social science. All three factors might have to be changed by the social scientist, independently of one another. Or it might suffice for the social scientist to change, say, only the structure on the assumption that manipulation of one factor will lead to a chain reaction of changes among the two remaining factors. The union-management example suggests that a forced change of behavior will lead to changes in modes of thought; the example of the chronically defeated group implies that planned changes in modes of thought and in structure will elicit changes in behavior. But social science has not yet worked out a formula for the appropriate sequence of change.

D. CHANGE: ITS DIRECTION AND MEASUREMENT

Change, of course, also comes about in business and industry by means other than the application of social science mode of thought and findings to specific problems, and the introduction of social inventions. Change is effected through changing market conditions, changing technology, changing availability of resources, and so on. Since we live in a dynamic rather than a static world, these changes are occurring simultaneously, along with whatever changes might be implemented through the efforts of social scientists or the acceptance of social science by businessmen. If proper use is to be made of social science, in this instance, in business and industry, the changes effected through it must be partialed out from changes occurring through other influences. Second, the actual degree of change brought about through application of social science must be measured, in order to understand just how effective social science might be in implementing change.

Third, should an application of social science not yield the expected change, this fact itself must be subject to systematic study in order to establish the factors which countervailed the social science application, thereby preventing the expected change to occur.

The problem of isolating factors which lead to change (or prevent planned change) and of measuring the degree of change is generic to social science. It must be solved if social science is to develop. Experimental findings are meaningless if extraneous factors have not been controlled and if the state of the subjects is not measured prior to the actual experiment, for example. The same holds for the effects of business training laboratories, reorganization for the improvement of human relations, and similar situations. Hence, both the businessman and the social scientist have a stake in the development of adequate methods for measuring change.

An Example from Insurance

There have been instances where business has applied social science knowledge in the hope of creating a change for the better without controlling for the influence of secular change or for the influence of extraneous factors, on what is to be changed. An example taken from the insurance business will illustrate the point. Insurance salesmen, in effect, intrude upon the privacy of a sales prospect.

Intrusion upon the privacy of others is not a "nice" way to behave in the United States; hence, insurance salesmen tend to react personally, with feelings of guilt, to the violation of privacy. Krugman suggests that this factor helps to account for the high rate of turnover among insurance salesmen. One insurance company provided its salesmen with acting lessons on the theory that such training would permit the salesmen to compartmentalize his feelings and to react in a depersonalized way to the violation of a prospect's privacy.[11]

The salesmen participated in the acting lessons as a group. Following the training program, turnover rates decreased among those who had participated. Although one could conclude that the training program had its desired effects, what is not clear is what aspect of the program contributed to the reduced turnover. Was it the acting lessons themselves or the fact that insurance salesmen had a chance to meet with each other, share common problems, and, in general, "blow steam" to release the accumulated tensions arising from interaction with prospects? For the insurance salesman usually works in isolation, using his home as office, has little contact with his colleagues, and so has little opportunity to discuss his business problems with others who have similar ones.[12]

To be able to establish conclusively whether the acting lessons *per se*, or the coming together with one's occupational colleagues, or a combination of the two factors contributed to reduced turnover one would need to study four aggregates of salesmen who have had comparable insurance careers. The first group would simply meet on a regular basis without acting lessons. Members of the second group would come together for acting lessons. The third would be given acting lessons individually and would not meet as a group. And the fourth aggregate would not be singled out in any way and would serve only as a control

---

11 Herbert E. Krugman, "Salesmen in Conflict: A Challenge to Marketing," *The Journal of Marketing*, July, 1958, p. 59.

12 Case cited by Paul Lazarsfeld in a seminar at Columbia University, Spring, 1962.

for comparison of turnover rates. With such a research design, one can assess the effectiveness of acting lessons in reducing turnover among insurance salesmen.[13]

Joint Diagnosis and Planning

To assess correctly the relevant factors which affect and effect a change and to evaluate the merits of a change require planning prior to implementation of the change factor itself. The key to planning is diagnosis of the problem jointly by management and the social scientist. Joint diagnosis and planning allows for adequate analysis of the system to be changed, for the design of an application which is suited to the particular problem, for mutual agreement on the degree of change which realistically might be expected, for provision of comprehensive before-and-after measurements which are sufficiently sensitive to detect even minute changes that might occur, and for making whatever preparations are necessary to minimize the emergence of a strain which might result through the introduction of a change factor into a business context.

Joint diagnosis and systematic planning of the proposed social science application have not always occurred in the past. This omission led many a management to suffer disenchantment with social science because it held vague utopian expectations about the changes which could be effected through the application of social science. Possibly one of the most crucial results of joint consultation prior to application is the emergence of a relatively realistic consensus between management and the social scientist on what can be expected in the way of change. Without the opportunity to formulate realistic expectations, management is tempted to anticipate dramatic results from the application of social science. Furthermore, joint consulta-

---

13 Krugman, *op. cit.*, p. 60.

tion permits management to involve itself in the proposed undertaking, thereby helping to reduce the feeling that the social scientist is attempting to run management's business.

To state the matter another way, the social scientist's responsibility extends beyond the designing and implementing of a change factor; he must also assume responsibility for the clarification of management's expectations prior to the application of the change factor. In this way, management's disappointment and subsequent disenchantment with social science can be mitigated to a considerable extent if the social science application were to yield only minute changes, or none at all. This double responsibility on the social scientist's part permits him to view his own plans for the proposed change with a degree of wariness and humility. For much research and experimentation are necessary to detect the flaws in a given application, and to eliminate these. Once management schools itself to expect realistic results rather than dramatic ones, the social scientist is under less pressure to treat his own work with awe and reverence.

The example of the human relations program will illustrate the point. The social scientists themselves are partially responsible for management's disillusionment with this application of social science. Management, concerned with the development of its human resources following World War II, essentially was permitted to accept human relations training as the gospel which would wash away all sins. And some social scientists helped perpetuate the view that human relations training is a gospel by not considering, or informing management, that the training program entailed certain risks since it had not been tested in a variety of circumstances. The experiences of the last decade and a half revealed the inadequacies of the program. While some businessmen might write these experiences off as failures, they represent "successes" for the social scientists. And those businessmen who employ a social science mode of thinking will recognize both the success and the failure. The failure is there because the businessman's investment did not bring him the returns he hoped to obtain. The success is there because the social scientist learned the limits of the human relations program through more practice with it, the conditions under which it does not pay off. Those companies that have learned along with the social scientists, and have overcome the disillusionment they experienced, now offer their employees human relations training with more reasonable expectations.

In short, the social scientist must be provided with, and take, sufficient opportunity to test his applications and "social inventions" in a variety of circumstances, thereby minimizing risks for the businessman, and providing him with some assurance that his social science investment has a high probability of bringing returns. At the same time, the businessman must develop more realistic expectations of what social science is able to do for him, and develop a willingness to take certain calculated risks in this area, just as he might in other areas, such as new product development.

The establishment of realistic expectations on management's part and the development of adequate applications and of adequate measuring instruments on the social scientist's part represent basic requirements for the effective use of social science in business, but by no means the only ones. An example of another *sine qua non*, and one which must be established early in the process of a social science application, is the creation of a receptive climate among the units to be involved in the application. The importance of a receptive climate can be illustrated by a negative example. A large motor company had some units surveyed by a polling agency without enlisting the units' cooperation ahead of time. The units had no choice in the matter nor any notion as to what might happen to them as a result of the survey findings. Consequently, no commitment to the survey was aroused; instead, defenses and negative reactions became apparent. Such a climate of feeling is not at all conducive to the acceptance of whatever changes management might have wanted to implement as a result of the survey.

In this particular instance, the data yielded by the survey led to only one change, namely, the announcement of workers' birthdays over the public address system in the cafeteria. No other changes were implemented because the agency conducting the survey had no notion of what the data meant. It proposed to the motor company that a study be made in order to provide information which would help in the data analysis, but the motor company at this point dropped the project. Although the agency was somewhat at fault for its inability to analyze the data on a meaningful level so that it could recommend other changes, the company was also at fault for not having specified clearly prior to the survey what it was interested in and why. Had adequate preparation been made prior to the survey, including the solicitation of cooperation from the units to be surveyed, the study might have led to more innovations than the announcement of birthdays.

The social scientist cannot be viewed as a fairy godmother who merely has to wave his magic questionnaire to implement a metamorphosis. By the same token, the businessman is not a Cinderella who gratefully accepts ephemeral changes. Both parties must realize that the business of change requires adequate preparation prior to implementation, just like any other business.

At this point the businessman might raise the traditional argument that he does not have the time to allow for adequate preparations prior to a study, the study itself, and finally, an implementation based on the results of a study. For he has to make decisions every day; therefore, he needs the answers now, not next year. Valid as this argument might be, it presents a one-sided short-range view of the situation. The businessman has to make a decision tomorrow, but he will also be making a decision ten years from now. The social scientist cannot provide an answer for tomorrow's decision, unless he happens to be familiar already with the problem at hand and has done prior research on it, but he can provide some answers for decisions that have to be made in the future.

Earlier we noted that the businessman as well as the social scientist can introduce change into a company. Change which is implemented initially through a manager's intuitive application of the social science mode of thought can also benefit from the social science method of evaluation. The manufacturing works of a metals company was under the rule of one man for twenty years. The man was autocratic, strongminded, and capable. Although the works was supposed to be a hierarchic organization, in practice it was extremely flat. Most subordinates reported to the works manager. At that time there was a seller's market, so the works was able to operate successfully despite its independent course as dictated by the manager and its dearth of relationships with other departments that usually provided services. When the manager retired, he was replaced by a dynamic man who felt that the company had never properly used its individual human resources. The new works manager, an engineer by training, intuitively felt that one had to work from the individual to the organization to make better use of the human factor. Furthermore, he believed that the changes he wanted to make could only be accomplished if his subordinates shared his attitudes. Hence, he replaced eight of the twelve department heads responsible to him before implementing his program. He attempted to clarify the organization's objectives and his own program of change. Once this was done, he was ready to turn to the important job of building better relations with other parts of the company. Since the market had changed from a seller's to a buyer's market, his job was not as simple as his predecessor's, and better relations with other departments would prove highly useful. He instigated weekly meetings with the department managers to discuss policies and problems, and he sent his personnel to such company-wide training activities as "sensitivity sessions."

Currently, a new manufacturing plant is under construction. The personnel to staff it have been selected from volunteers working in existing plants. These persons are being trained in "family sensitivity sessions" before assuming responsibility for the unit. As a result of the involvement of these men, there already has been an increase in the overall effectiveness of the organization. Active participation of more individuals, coupled with more skilled applications to manufacturing problems, has led to substantial technical improvements and higher productivity. Another consequence was that the works itself has become less tradition-minded, no longer accepting something because it was there yesterday.

The company itself has a feeling that there has been progress in its overall effectiveness, but does not have sufficient tangible evidence to date to support this. Answers to these questions are important, for the company, now that it has embarked upon a new program, is asking what else can be done to facilitate change and to make better use of human resources. Answers to these questions would enable it to decide what to add to the program, whether or not to speed it up, and so forth.

In essence then, this metals company embarked upon

a program of change because one high-ranking employee intuitively used the social science mode of thinking and acted upon it. But one can only go so far in effecting change with just a social science mode of thinking. There comes a time when the other uses of social science must be called upon, if the dynamics of the change are to be understood, and if more change is to occur. Thus once again we have been brought full circle, from the social science mode of thought to problems of measuring change.

E. SOCIAL SCIENCE AS A SOURCE OF TRAINING

In this age of specialization, the social scientist exercises a virtual monopoly on the development of social science findings and their application, and on the techniques used in evaluating progress and change. This monopoly is not easy to break for the simple reason that the ability to use these skills requires a lengthy training period which is usually obtained within social science departments of graduate schools. As we have indicated before, however, the social scientist does not have a monopoly on his way of thought, for others can employ it intuitively. Moreover, the social science mode of thought is relatively easily accessible by reading books, taking a course, or using other devices which force one to think more systematically about human behavior.

Given the proper opportunity then, the businessman can learn to use the social science mode of thought, or if he already uses it intuitively, can receive reassurance about his ideas. In recent years the Ford Foundation has taken an interest in this problem, and through its inspiration and sponsorship, business schools are beginning to include in their curricula social science courses taught by social scientists.

These social science courses are not geared to finding

the correct answer for a specific problem which might arise in business, but instead are oriented toward the larger implications and generalizations which underlie the correct answer. Again, an example will clarify the point.

At the Harvard School of Business, a specific case which describes a business problem is presented to the students. The students are expected to discuss the problem and to make a decision as to its correct resolution. Essentially, they are expected to assume the role of a businessman faced with this problem and make a businessman's decision with regard to it. A typical problem is as follows. The organization in question has a regional division head, and under him, a manager at level 1 and one at level 2. A relatively high position is now vacant. The two managers discuss the possibilities of selecting for the job one of several persons who are eligible for promotion. Since there is disagreement over one particular candidate for the job, the managers present the disagreement to the regional head who resolves the problem.

The disagreement stems from differing evaluations of the candidate. Manager 1 perceives the employee as a skilled person and a good chemist who takes evening courses to keep abreast of developments in his field. Manager 2 sees that the individual lacks neatness about his person, is stubborn about his opinions, and will not listen to others. Moreover, since he has many union contacts he is likely to become a troublemaker. The businessman might be interested only in how to resolve the dispute between the two managers, and yet pick the best man for the job. But the social scientist is interested in the factors which led to the decision.

The social scientist notes that Manager 1, who is responsible for the completion of the tasks which go with the now vacant position, emphasizes competency. Manager 2 perceives the vacant position as a stepping stone to the top, and so stresses "social" attributes. Thus the managers judge the suitability of a person for a given position on the basis of how the position relates to their particular roles or perceptions. In short, the social scientist analyzes the frame of reference from which a person makes a decision or an evaluation. Once the frame of reference is understood, one can study factors which determine it, and so get at the underlying aspects of decision making that are not generally known and often taken for granted.

With regard to the resolution of the problem at hand, whether or not the sloppy but competent chemist should be promoted, the decision depends upon how the top management defines the vacant position and the purpose of the promotion. If the regional head is concerned with having the position competently filled, then he might favor the person in question. But if he wants to groom someone for future promotions, then most likely he would look for someone else to fill the job. Thus the social scientist is not so much concerned with actual decision as is the businessman, but with the ultimate base for making a decision.

This last statement can be generalized as follows. The social scientist is not so much concerned with action *per se*, but with the factors that underly a given act. Here we must differentiate between the various social sciences. The psychologist is concerned with factors inherent in the individual which lead to a particular act, while the sociologist is concerned with factors inherent in roles and situations which lead to a particular act. These general statements apply to all the cases presented above. By analyzing the factors which lead to competitive acts between groups, for example, one begins to see a way of avoiding intergroup competition.

Once the businessman has acquired a social science mode of thought, whether through business school courses or by other means; he can use it in his day-to-day decisions.

Even so, the social science mode of thought might not be able to solve all the businessman's "people" problems for him. For some problems he will have to turn to the social scientist himself to obtain the benefit of specific findings and techniques of evaluation and measurement. And even then, social science, given its present state of development, might only be able to solve *some* problems, but not *all*.

IV. Implementation of Social Science Knowledge

THE IMPLEMENTATION of social science knowledge links knowledge and action by translating social science findings into an action program. Given the data provided by the social scientists' research studies, how are these data used by an industrial organization? Industrial organizations have developed mechanisms for implementing research findings from the physical sciences. Industry consistently utilizes the findings from the physical scientists who work in universities and laboratories. Units and departments that specialize in determining the practical uses of the research of the physical scientist are established in industrial organizations. But there is no counterpart of this in the social sciences; there is virtually no similar machinery for developing and testing the application of social ideas.

Some social scientists maintain that it is not part of their professional role to ascertain the practical uses of their research. One example of this is the case of a social scientist who limited his professional role to making a survey and reporting the results of the survey to his client. When the first steam laundry opened in Vienna, few women used it. The social scientist was commissioned to do a study of what was wrong. He made a survey of the few women who did use the steam laundry to determine why and in what situations they patronized it in order to get a clue as to why other women did not use it. He found that the women distrusted this innovation; the middle class Viennese housewives felt that doing laundry at home was part of their feminine role and gave them power in the household. They used the steam laundry only in an emergency such as illness in the family (though a few continued to patronize it after their first experience with it). The social scientist wrote a report stating the reasons why the steam laundry was not being used widely, but he felt that it was not his business to interpret the findings. However, the laundry owner devised a way to utilize his research findings. The laundry owner reasoned that family deaths qualify as emergencies. He began to check the obituary columns in the newspapers each day, and sent sympathetic letters advertising his services to those families in which there had been a death. This proved to be very effective and business flourished for the steam laundry.

Some social scientists feel that they are not responsible for determining the practical uses of their research. Other social scientists feel that they do not know how to implement their findings; they lack the skills needed to translate research findings into action programs. Very little training in social engineering is given to social scientists, and only a few have had practical experience in implementing their knowledge.

Some social scientists argue that the person who is talented in analyzing situations and conducting research may not have the talent to implement findings or translate them into an action program. One solution which has been suggested is to have a specially trained person, a third party, who takes the research findings of the social scientist and ascertains how they can be utilized by the manager in the organization.

Implementing the research findings of the social scientists is a particularly crucial problem where research cannot be undertaken unless its practical uses have been determined beforehand. For example, the administrator in charge of social science in the Office of Naval Research has to know how he is going to use the research findings in order to justify getting the money to undertake the research initially.

In a few cases social science data can be easily translated into an action program for the company. For example, one company changed its course of action with regard to its union contract as a result of the findings from a social science survey of workers. The company was concerned with the kind of package it would offer the workers in the forthcoming union contract. One item the company's management intended to include in the package was an increase in life insurance which it thought would be well received by the workers. A survey was made of the workers' actual aspirations, preference, and expectations. One unexpected finding in the survey was that additional life insurance would mean nothing to the workers. Most workers had very little idea of how much life insurance the company was currently giving them, and they wanted only 10 per cent of the life insurance they presently had. All that the workers wanted was enough life insurance to cover their burial expenses and to leave their wives $1,000.00 or so. As a result of the survey, the managers changed the package offer they had intended to give the workers. They deleted the additional life insurance and substituted for it something the workers had said they definitely wanted.

The Feedback Method for Creating Organizational Change

One mechanism which has been developed to utilize the research findings of the social scientist in the organization is the feedback process as used by Floyd Mann in his relationship with Detroit Edison Company. Though there are many different systems, this particular feedback process was specifically developed as a mechanism for instituting organizational change through the utilization of social science findings. This particular process of feedback involves confronting organizational personnel—first managers and then employees—with social science facts in several different stages each of which is successively less distant from the individual personally. People are given feedback of their performance which serves as standards against which they can change. This process attempts to get people in an organization to start thinking about social science facts and to show them how such facts (such as attitudes toward work or relationships with supervisors) are related to their philosophy.

This feedback process was developed by Floyd Mann of the Survey Research Center while he was doing research on organizational processes at Detroit Edison. The fifteen-year relationship between social scientists from the Survey Research Center and Detroit Edison was described in Chapter II and was an important ingredient in the development of and effectiveness of the feedback process. The effective working relations between the social scientists and the managers made it possible for the social scientists to conduct several research studies over time in which they could measure change. Moreover, they had access to employees at all levels in the organization who received feedback from the findings of these studies.

The feedback process is designed to work within a hierarchical power structure and with the line personnel. The feedback is introduced within a regular problem-solving unit in the organizational hierarchy—what Mann calls the "organizational family"—the superior and his immediate subordinates. In using the feedback process within the hierarchical power structure, the researcher works with successively lower groups within the organization. For example, if the feedback process were to be introduced successfully in a small company, it would be necessary to begin the process with the top organizational family—the president and the members of that unit which holds the power and makes the major decisions. Otherwise, the feedback process could be expected to flounder and eventually fail due to the different and conflicting philosophies the various members of such a unit hold because of their respective roles.

How does the feedback process operate? Managers and supervisory personnel are shown several successive profiles of social science data related to their working environment. The profile of data is like a mirror in that the data which are directly relevant to and of interest to the individual reflect the attitudes and relationships involved in the immediate working situation. Each successive profile of data that is fed back to the individual is more closely related to his personal working situation and his own performance. For example, the first data shown a group of supervisors may involve the attitudes of subordinates toward their supervisors from another company. The second profile may show the past attitudes that subordinates in their company held toward supervisors.

Eventually, the supervisors are shown data on what the attitudes of their own subordinates currently are toward them. The supervisors are given the opportunity to see how they are perceived by their subordinates, which in many cases will lead to changes in their behavior or at least to a greater understanding of the problems and conflicts involved in their relationship with subordinates. Individuals do not always accept the facts with which they are presented. Moreover, one cannot expect them to make many changes since many individuals have fairly stereotyped behavior patterns and stereotypic opinions of others. This rigidity on the part of a person is a problem for he may fail to see changes in another person's behavior and may continue to react according to his stereotyped image of the other person.

To illustrate how the feedback process proceeded in one company an example in which it was used will be given. The social scientist was concerned with an "organizational family" which was not working effectively together, and used the feedback process in an attempt to shape the family into a team that would solve problems together.

Data were collected for an "organizational family," which is a group of interlocking, face-to-face groups within the organizational hierarchy. The subordinate in one group is the superordinate in another group as in the case of the position of supervisor. The supervisor represents the bridge which connects two divergent groups.

In this case the organizational family recognized the need for team work, but there was very little of this among its members. Problem-solving meetings were held in which the social scientist acted as resource man and sat at the end of the room. The supervisors tossed around ideas, but the social scientist participated only when questions were asked of him or there was a need for him to break down and explain the findings that were being presented.

The mirror is held far away at first with data from another company given to the supervisors. However, they are resistant to accepting data from other companies as they "know" that their company is different.

Then findings on the attitudes of their subordinates toward them several years before are given to them. An example of this might be the percentage of employees in high production units that say the supervisor is good at handling people. Some supervisors react by saying that subordinates do not have the right to evaluate them. At this point one needs to make the supervisor identify with the rank and file in order for him to accept the data. By demonstrating analogous data from his level, where he is placed in the position of subordinate vis-à-vis his superiors, he begins to see the similarities between his subordinates and himself. At this point data are given on how people at his level, the supervisors, evaluate their superiors. From this he sees the similarity between his attitudes toward his superior and the attitudes of his subordinates toward him and the data begin to make sense. The mirror has been moved in more closely toward the individual supervisor. He begins to see that his subordinates have certain rights just as he feels that he as a supervisor has certain rights with respect to his superordinates.

Having accepted the several levels of older data that have been presented, the supervisors want to see data that reflect the current attitudes of their subordinates. At this point, current data which compare supervisors from similar units showing the difference between them are fed back. The data are related to the productivity of the unit and many supervisors are shocked by the data.

The only time that data are not presented within the problem-solving unit is when the profile of an individual is explained to him in more detail. The individual's profile is broken down for him, to show him how well he does on specific items that he as a group member identified as important to see. It is presented to him individually to protect him and to allow him to change his operations before his superior knows about his inadequacies. The data are not necessarily believed or accepted by all individuals. In many cases, the supervisors do not see the difference between items. For example, one man was scored high by his subordinates on the question "Do subordinates feel free to bring problems to him?" but he was scored low on the question "Do subordinates feel that he asks them for opinions?" The supervisor thought that the items were the same and wondered out loud why he had scored high on the first and low on the second. Giving him a lecturette would not help, but by using reflective and nondirective counseling techniques it is possible to get the employee to think and talk about how he relates to others. He then begins to understand and see how the findings describe his behavior as others see him, and to accept the findings. In this instance the man's response was, "Could it be that I snap off answers about business, but if a guy comes to me about personal problems, we have coffee together."

By starting with the mirror far away from the individual and gradually bringing it closer, the person has a chance to understand the meaning of the data without being personally threatened. Moreover, since the people who participate in the feedback process work together on a daily basis, when the data are presented in this way it does not disrupt the on-going relationships by being too personal or threatening to the group members.

The feedback process is one mechanism that has been developed and successfully used to bring back the findings from social science research to the level of the individual employee in such a way that changes in personal attitudes and behavior are possible. The social scientist collects the facts and makes his studies, after which he reports the findings back to the organization reaching individuals at all levels in the hierarchy.

T-Group Methods of Changing Attitudes and Behavior

Another successful method of changing the attitudes and behavior of individuals in industry is the "T" (training) groups or "sensitivity sessions." The T-group approach was developed by the National Training Laboratories. The method evolved from several traditions in social science, in particular, the work of Kurt Lewin and the group dynamics school. Great advances in the application of social science were initiated in 1958 by Esso's experiments in the use of laboratory methods for management development.

The T-group approach is a means of sensitizing businessmen to interpersonal and intergroup relations problems which may arise in their working relationships. A T-group session consists of businessmen sitting around a table and going through the process of establishing communication, becoming acquainted, recognizing problems, and working out interpersonal conflicts. The T-group trainer is a social scientist who acts as a consultant during the sessions.

The original T-groups were "stranger" groups consisting of persons who did not know each other previously and would not necessarily have a future together after the sessions. In the stranger group, the social scientist trainer has the authority. Here the individuals learn a great deal about themselves personally, and significant changes occur in individual attitudes and behavior.

Within the last few years, other kinds of T-groups have been developed. These include "family" groups and "cousin" groups. Family groups are composed of members who work together in an organization including supervisors and their subordinates. The cousin group draws from a diagonal slice through an organization by taking supervisors and subordinates from different levels in the hierarchy. For example, the head of one department, the assistant head of a second department, and the supervisor of a third department may be found in a cousin group.

The target of change in the stranger groups is the individual. With the use of family and cousin groups, the target of change is broadened to include organizational units and departments. Even though individual changes were made in stranger groups, the changes tended to disappear over time because of the fade-out effect. Members from stranger groups would return to their organizations, but they lacked support from people with similar experiences, so the effects of the T-group would wear off over time. In family and cousin groups, however, long-term organizational changes can be made in units and departments, since the T-group members who continue to work together after the experience can give support and reinforcement to each other.

In family groups, the focus is on clarifying expectations and shared perceptions. Members of these groups become aware of such things as the need to improve certain relationships or the realization that other people can be helpful in the work situation. This provides a basis for improvement of future working relationships. If the members of a family group have homogenous values, the group is less successful for there is less opportunity to learn to respect different perspectives and values.

The relationship between the boss and his subordinates can affect the success of a family group session. Even if the boss is disliked or considered to be a hardhead by his subordinates, after an initial period of resistance members of the family group will usually establish effective communication and work out their problems. However, if the boss is basically distrusted by his subordinates, it is difficult to break through this distrust and the session is likely to be less successful.

The art of the trainer, however, is largely one of refusing to accept the "leader" role which members would like to force upon him. Few managers, by disposition or training, are likely to be able to decline the dominant role.

V. Summary and Conclusion

AT THE OUTSET of this report we made an analogy to flirtation and courtship in order to describe the pre- and post-World War II relations between the social sciences on the one hand, and business and industry on the other. Now, possibly the time is ripe for a relationship between social science and business which is as serious and long lasting as marriage. This report might be viewed as an effort to contribute to the emergence of a long and stable relationship between the two parties.

For viable relations to develop between two persons each must become familiar with the needs and expectations of the other. In the first chapter we described the needs and expectations of both the social scientist and the businessman. We indicated how differences with regard to needs and expectations could create conflict potentially, unless the two parties mutually defined their expectations. Finally, we gave an example of a successful relationship between social science and business, the Survey Research Center and Detroit Edison, to show that consensus about a situation is not achieved immediately but requires the close cooperation of both parties for an extended period of time.

Presumably the *raison d'etre* for establishing a relationship between social science and business is that each can benefit from the other. The social scientist benefits because the businessman can provide research sites. The businessman benefits because the application of social science knowledge contributes to a more effective operation of his enterprise. In the second chapter we have sketched out some general uses of social science in business and described some specific applications which have been made. These uses range from social science as a mode of thinking which might help the businessman in his day-to-day activities to the development of programs which help reduce conflict between organizational units.

Returning to our marital analogy, even though husband and wife have established a stable relationship through consensus on the definition of the situation and the establishment of reciprocity, there remains one more problem, namely, how to raise children should they decide to start a family. Within certain limits the actual implementation of social science knowledge, which we discuss in the last chapter, is analogous to rearing a child. For implementation involves third parties, i.e., the personnel of the unit who are to receive the social science application. If parents are to raise their children successfully, they must exercise a certain degree of caution and foresight. By the same token, if the social science application is to be successful, the scientist and the businessman must exercise care in its implementation. In the last chapter we describe some problems relating to implementation, and again, use the case of Detroit Edison to illustrate one method for successful implementation.

There are two general sociological themes which underlie the various facets of our report. One is what sociologists call "the norm of reciprocity." This norm, or expectation for behavior, has a broader meaning than the old adage that one can't get something for nothing. In the course of working together neither the businessman nor the social scientist gets something for nothing. Both benefit in a very concrete sense, but in order for an exchange of benefits to occur, each must become involved and to some degree committed to the problems and concerns of the other. Thus, a viable relationship not only is based on direct exchange (e.g., research sites for application and implementation) but is also based on a more subtle exchange —namely, involvement with each other's interests. This subtle form of exchange should also extend to third parties, to the personnel who are the object of change. Employees, unlike machines, do not respond automatically when a new switch is installed or a new program is fed in. To elicit their cooperation, their involvement in the implementation process should be solicited. This can be done best by showing a concern for the problems of the employees, and in turn, permitting them to become concerned with the problems and interests of the social scientist and of the businessman. It is the establishment of the more subtle aspects of the norm of reciprocity, those which tap feelings of involvement and commitment, which will facilitate the emergence of satisfactory relations between the social scientist and the businessman, and also contribute to the successful implementation of social science knowledge.

The second general sociological theme underlying our discussion is that the norms of a group are both the means and ends of social change. Research in a variety of contexts, which include juvenile gangs and prison communities as well as experimental groups, has indicated that if change is to be effected in individuals, the norms of the group to which they belong and with which they identify must be changed. Throughout this report, implicitly or explicitly, we have talked about the need to change norms or the need to establish new norms. The viability of the emergent relationship between the social scientist and the businessman depends on the formation of new norms which are more appropriate to their situation. The application of social science knowledge in many instances consists of redefining the norms which govern action. Finally, if the application is to be implemented successfully, other norms must be introduced to ease the transition from the old situation to the new one.

Just as social science cannot be treated as an automatic panacea for the problems of business and industry, so this report cannot be viewed as a panacea for the problems which beset the uses of social science in business and industry. At best, we have outlined the areas in which the social scientist and the businessman should strive to cooperate, and have indicated a few methods for cooperation based on past experiences of social scientists and businessmen.

Social science has often been compared to natural science in an effort both to legitimate and to debunk the former. In the final analysis, social science has to be legitimated or debunked on its own merits. But certain kinds of comparisons between social science and natural science could prove fruitful. The natural sciences, with their longer history, have solved or are closer to solving problems which the social sciences are now facing. One problem is that of the relationship between the natural scientists and businessmen. The natural scientist, like his social counterpart, is often the marginal man in industry. Likewise, the natural scientist tends to be more concerned with basic research than with applied research. In short, many of the dilemmas and problems which we described in the first chapter hold or have held for the natural scientist as well as for the social scientist. Given this fact, plus the fact that business and industry looked to the natural sciences for assistance long before they looked to the social sciences, it suggests that social scientists should study the emergent relations

between natural science and business in order to understand their own problems better. The natural scientist and
the businessman might well have evolved ways of relating
to each other and ways of utilizing the knowledge of natural science in business which could be of value to the social
scientist and the businessman.

BIBLIOGRAPHY

ADAMS, J. S. "Toward an Understanding of Inequity." Behavioral Research Service, General Electric Company.

ADAMS, J. S., and ROSENBAUM, W. B. "The Relationship of Worker Productivity to Cognitive Dissonance about Wage Inequities." Behavioral Research Service, General Electric Company.

ADAMS, R. N., and PREISS, J. H. (eds.). *Human Organization Research*. Homewood, Illinois: The Dorsey Press, Inc., 1960.

ALLEN, LOUIS A. "Does Management Development Develop Manager," *Personnel,* Vol. XXXIV (September–October, 1957), pp. 18-25.

ANDREWS, KENNETH R. "Is Management Training Effective?" *Harvard Business Review,* No. 1 (January–February, 1957), pp. 85-94; *ibid.,* No. 2 (March–April, 1957), pp. 63-72.

ARGYRIS, CHRIS. "Explorations in Consulting Client Relationships," *Human Organizations,* Vol. 20, No. 3 (1961), pp. 121-133.

————. *Interpersonal Competence and Organizational Effectiveness*. Homewood, Illinois: Richard D. Irwin, Inc. and The Dorsey Press, Inc., 1962.

————. *Understanding Organizational Behavior*. Homewood, Illinois: The Dorsey Press, Inc., 1962.

BARITZ, LOREN. *The Servants of Power*. Middletown: Wesleyan University Press.

BENNE, K. D., and SWANSON, G. E. "The Problem of Values and the Social Sciences," *Journal of Social Issues,* Vol. 6, No. 4, (1950), pp. 2-7.

BENNIS, W. G. "Revisionist Theory of Leadership," *Harvard Business Review,* Vol. 39 (1961), pp. 26-36, 146-50.

75

BENNIS, W. B.; BENNE, K., and CHIN, R. *The Planning of Change.* New York: Holt, Rinehart & Winston, 1961.

CARLSON, ROBERT O. "On the Prevalence of Crypto-Social Science Research in Industry." New York: Standard Oil Company (New Jersey). Paper read at the Association for the Study of Social Problems meeting, St. Louis, Missouri, August, 1961.

CARTWRIGHT, D. "Basic and Applied Social Psychology," *Philosophy of Science,* Vol. 16, No. 3 (1949), pp. 198-208.

————. *Studies in Social Power.* Ann Arbor: Institute for Social Research.

CARTWRIGHT, D., and ZANDER, A. *Group Dynamics.* Rev. ed.; New York: Row, Peterson & Co., 1960.

CHAPPLE, E. D., and SAYLES, L. R. *The Measure of Management: Designing Organizations for Human Effectiveness.* New York: Macmillan Co., 1961.

CHEIN, I.; COOK, S. W., and HARDING, J. "The Use of Research in Social Therapy," *Human Relations,* Vol. 1 (1948), pp. 512-32.

CYERT, R. M.; DILL, W. R., and MARCH, J. G. "The Role Expectations in Business Decision Making," *Administrative Science Quarterly,* Vol. III (December, 1958), pp. 306-40.

DAHL, R. G.; HAIRE, M., and LAZARSFIELD, P. F. *Social Science Research on Business: Product and Potential.* New York: Columbia University Press, 1959.

DIMOCK, MARSHALL E. *A Philosophy of Administration.* New York: Harper & Bros., 1958.

————. *Administrative Vitality: The Conflict with Bureaucracy.* New York: Harper & Bros., 1959.

ETZIONI, AMITAI. *Complex Organizations, a Sociological Reader.* New York: Holt, Rinehart & Winston, Inc., 1961. In particular, Part II which contains several articles evaluating the human relations traditions, and the article by Bernard Levenson, "Bureaucratic Succession," which is concerned with problems of promotion.

————. *A Comparative Analysis of Complex Organizations.* New York: The Free Press of Glencoe, 1961; especially pp. 31-39, 113-26, 165-68, 175-98.

FESTINGER, LEON, and KATZ, DANIEL. *Research Methods in the Behavioral Sciences.* New York: The Dryden Press, 1953.

GOODE, W. J., and FOWLER, I. "Incentive Factors in a Low-morale Plant," *American Sociological Review,* Vol. 14 (1949), pp. 618-24.

GORDON, R. A., and HOWELL, J. E. *Higher Education for Business.* New York: Columbia University Press, 1959.

GOULDNER, ALVIN. *Patterns of Industrial Bureaucracy.* Glencoe, Illinois: The Free Press, 1954. In particular, see the appendix.

GUETZKOW, HAROLD. "Conversion Barriers in Using the Social Sciences," *Administrative Science Quarterly,* Vol. 4, No. 1 (1959), pp. 68-81.

GUEST, ROBERT H. *Organizational Change: The Effect of Successful Leadership.* Homewood, Illinois: Richard D. Irwin, Inc. and The Dorsey Press, Inc., 1962. This study continues in the Human Relations tradition. The question which the reader must keep in mind is why it was effective in the particular organization studied.

KAHN, R. L., and MANN, F. C. "Uses of Survey Research in Policy Determination," *Proceedings of the Ninth Annual Meeting of Industrial Relations Research Association,* No. 18 (December, 1956), pp. 256-74.

LAZARSFELD, PAUL F., and THIELENS, JR., W. *The Academic Mind.* Glencoe, Illinois: The Free Press, 1958, pp. 12-14, 226-27, 246, 395.

LEAVITT, H. J. *Managerial Psychology: An Introduction to Individuals, Pairs and Groups in Organizations.* Chicago: University of Chicago Press, 1958.

LIKERT, RENSIS. *New Patterns of Management.* New York: McGraw-Hill Book Co., Inc., 1960.

LIKERT, RENSIS, and LIPPITT, RONALD. The utilization of social science in Leon Festinger and Daniel Katz (eds.), *Research Methods in the Behavioral Sciences.* New York: The Dryden Press, 1953.

LIPPITT, R. "The Strategy of Sociopsychological Research," in J. G. Miller (ed.), *Experiments in Social Process.* New York: McGraw-Hill Book Co., Inc., 1950, pp. 17-30.

LIPPITT, R.; WATSON, J., and WESTLEY, B. *The Dynamics of Planned Change.* New York: Harcourt Brace & Co., 1959.

MCGREGOR, DOUGLAS. *The Human Side of Enterprise.* New York: McGraw-Hill Book Co., Inc., 1960.

McGregor, D.; Knickbocker, I.; Haire, M., and Bavelas, A. "The Consultant Role and Organizational Leadership," *Journal of Social Issues,* 1948.

Mann, F. C. "Human Relations Skills in Social Research," *Human Relations,* Vol. 4 (1951), pp. 341-54.

Mann, F. C., and Baumgartel, H. *Absences and Employee Attitudes in an Electrical Power Company.* Ann Arbor, Michigan: Institute for Social Research, 1953.

Mann, F. C., and Dent, J. *Appraisals of Supervisors.* Ann Arbor, Michigan: Survey Research Center, University of Michigan, 1954.

Mann, F. C., and Hoffman, L. R. *Automation and the Worker: A Study of Social Change.* New York: Henry Holt, 1960.

Mann, F. C., and Likert, R. "The Need for Research on Communicating Research Results," *Human Organization,* Vol. 11, No. 4 (1952), pp. 15-19.

Mann, F. C., and Neff, Franklin. *Managing Major Change in Organizations.* Rev. ed.; Ann Arbor, Michigan: Foundation for Research on Human Behavior, 1962.

Mann, F. C., and Williams, L. K. "Dynamics of a Change to Electronic Data-Processing Equipment," *Administrative Science Quarterly,* Vol. V (September, 1960), pp. 217-56.

Marcson, Simon. *The Scientist in American Industry: Some Organizational Determinants in Manpower Utilization.* New York: Harper, 1960.

Merton, Robert K. "The Machine, the Worker and the Engineer," in *Social Theory and Social Structure.* Glencoe, Illinois: The Free Press, 1957.

Schacter, Stanley, *et al.* "Emotional Disruption and Industrial Productivity," *Journal of Applied Psychology,* Vol. 45 (1961), pp. 201-13. Description of an experiment conducted by the Behavioral Research Service of the General Electric Company.

Seashore, S.; Lippitt, R., and Gibb, J. "A Study of Communication of Theory in a Human Relations Laboratory," Ann Arbor, Michigan: Foundation for Research in Human Behavior, March, 1962, mimeographed report.

Selltiz, C.; Jahoda, M.; Deutsch, M., and Cook, S. W. *Research Methods in Social Relations.* Rev. ed.; New York: Henry Holt & Co., 1960.

SHEPARD, H. A. "Nine Dilemmas in Industrial Research," *Administrative Science Quarterly,* Vol. I (December, 1956), pp. 295-309.

SHEPARD, H. A., and BLAKE, R. R. "Changing Behavior Through Cognitive Change," *Human Organization,* supplement, 1962.

SHERIF, MUZAFER. "Experiments in Group Conflict," *Scientific American,* November, 1956.

SOFER, CYRIL. *The Organization from Within: A Comparative Study of Social Institutions Based on a Sociotherapeutic Approach.* London: Tavistock Institute, 1961.

STROTHER, G. B. (ed.). *Social Science Approaches to Business Behavior.* Homewood, Illinois: Richard D. Irwin, Inc. and The Dorsey Press, Inc., 1962.

ZETTERBERG, HANS L. *Social Theory and Social Practice.* New York: The Bedminister Press, 1962. A program is put forth as a means for bridging the gap between social science knowledge and its application to problems.

PARTICIPANTS

RALPH H. BOWLES
*Manager of Manpower
Research*

GENESCO

J. D. BROOKS
*Research Associate
Organization Planning*

United States Steel Corporation

R. M. DECKER
*Training Development
Department*

Western Electric Company, Inc.

JAMIE DENNIS
Personnel Research

Humble Oil and Refining Company

HORACE DePODWIN
Manager, Public Affairs Research and Planning Service

General Electric Company

RICHARD C. DRESSER
Special Projects Editor

Appleton-Century-Crofts, Inc.

STEPHEN JECKOVICH
*General Manager
Production Services*

The Pittsburgh Plate Glass Company

JOHN PAUL JONES
*General Manager
Organization Development*

Union Carbide Corporation

JEROME F. KIRK
*Industrial Relations
Special Projects Department*

Ford Motor Company

H. S. LADD   Aluminum Company of Canada,
Assistant Works Manager   Ltd.
Kingston Works

PAUL F. LAZARSFELD   Columbia University
Department of Sociology

SVEN LUNDSTEDT   Foundation for Research on Hu-
Assistant Director   man Behavior

FLOYD C. MANN   University of Michigan
Professor of Psychology

W. P. MATHERS   The Bell Telephone Company of
Assistant Vice President   Pennsylvania

JAMES MILAM   The Boeing Company
Assistant to the Director of
Industrial Relations
Aero Space Division

HOLLIS W. PETER   Foundation for Research on Hu-
Director   man Behavior

J. W. PORTER   Sun Oil Company
Director of Personnel
Development

F. L. W. RICHARDSON, JR.   University of Pittsburgh
School of Business Adminis-
tration

LANE RILAND   Eastman Kodak Company
Industrial Psychologist

J. R. SCHMITT   Olin Mathieson Chemical Corp.
Executive Placement Officer

M. J. SHANNON   Western Electric Company, Inc.

HERBERT A. SHEPARD   Case Institute of Technology
Professor of Behavioral
Science

RENATO TAGIURI   Harvard University
Graduate School of Business
Administration

THOMAS A. VAN TRIES   Mountain States Telephone and
Vice President—Personnel   Telegraph Company

FRANKLYN WALTMAN
Director
Public Relations Department

Sun Oil Company

GOODWIN WATSON
Professor of Education

Columbia University

Index

*This book has been set on the Linotype
in 12 point and 10 point Times Roman,
leaded 2 points. Chapter numbers and
titles are in 18 point Craw Clarendon
Book. The size of the type page is 24
by 43 picas.*